White Nightgown

Poems

White Nightgown

Poems

Megan Gannon

Apprentice
House Press
Loyola University Maryland

First Edition

Printed in the United States of America

Paperback ISBN: 978-1-62720-033-2
Ebook ISBN: 978-1-62720-034-9

Design by Andrew Grahn

Apprentice House
Loyola University Maryland
4501 N. Charles Street
Baltimore, MD 21210
410.617.5265 • 410.617.2198 (fax)
www.ApprenticeHouse.com
info@ApprenticeHouse.com

For Manny

Acknowledgements

Best American Poetry 2006—"Westering" as "List of First Lines"

Crazyhorse— "Definition," "Deep Sea"

Gulf Coast— "White Nightgown"

Laurel Review—"Testament"

Louisville Review—"Sonnet"

New Orleans Review—"Shade"

Notre Dame Review— "The Names of Birds," "Etymology of Evening"

Pleiades— "Atlantean"

Poetry Daily March 2, 2007— "She Wearies of Wise Children"

Poetry Kanto (Japan)—"Eve's Excuse" as "First Excuse," "Adam's Defense"as "First Defense," "Late April," "Well Water," "Go back" as "Monologue"

Seneca Review—"Aquifer"

Sweet; A Literary Confection—"You Were Not There," "History," "Vows"

Sonora Review—"Myth"

Third Coast—"Westering"as "List of First Lines," "Selenographia," "She Wearies of Wise Children"

The Untidy Season; An Anthology of Nebraska Women Poets— "Weather," "Dungeness," "The Dead, Dreaming," "Daphne Digging In"

Verse Daily April 26, 2006—"Testament;" December 17, 2008—"Adam's Defense"as "First Defense"

Table of Contents

Go back before the body [   ]
                    who borrows your breath
[   ] and leaves you— [   ]
                    before the dream of falling,
drowning, drifting—
                    dream of your life as you've lived it.

Deep Sea

What does the band
sound like in water
waking, the tempo a changing
wave that gathers and releases as it
fills? See, a doorknob
drifts down, and one by one the hundreds
of china cups upright
for how far, falling. Hours,
now everyone moves
gracefully; now we have some place
to put our dead. How many
pressures their bodies get used to,
the slender necks
of bottles, emerald, intact.
Without air, they hardly know
how wetly they're under us,
how the verdigrised currents
churn sediment, cracking
watch-faces and tugging laces
loose. In the dream-
coursing that clogs ears,
the greeny-grey where
metal drips and ball-gowns
bloom, whatever wounds
they've acquired washed
white, skin-flaps
sealed like fishy lips.

Selenographia

Some of you is lodged,
                must be,

somewhere between the sea
of serenity, or the lake of sleep,
or the marsh of sleep, or the sea.

Particles of solar wind, caught,
some whisker of skin fishings,
                I don't know.
                I hope not
the sea of cold.
There was so little of you,

barely enough for the buried

crystalline drops we know now
are there, hardly
an ocean of storms.
                Honestly,

I know there's an eye
brightening even when its full
waning's waned,
                albedo of coal,
                light of ice,

but I can't feel it.

Fingers caught in the classroom
door's heavy hinge, how your sound
                        tore through me,
knocking loose some stray ovum,
sea of crises, sea of fecundity,

risen and hovering,
not every sound keeps traveling,
some stay, like stoned gall,
bay of seething, straight through

to the bay of the center.
When that shriek descended
to the newly kaleidoscoped car,
many-faceted geodesic dome that propelled you

                somewhere,
sea of rains, sea of vapors,

I was no known sea.

                How the word
for indigo churning with its back to us means
noting all along at a certain distance.
                Now complex eye.

Up there, the air's so thin
it can't be mimicked, even in our best vacuum.
Down here, it's the weight of two boots
on my sternum. Must you
keep orbiting at this
mean distance?

What doesn't descend,
　　　shouldn't. If I hadn't heard
even some of the words, you wouldn't.

_____ you _____ Kyle?
He was _____ in a car _____.

I won't accept this moon illusion—
a thing's not bigger riding the horizon.
There's only so long I'll let these
high tides pull.

　　　　　<u>Are</u> you <u>there</u>, Kyle?
　　　　　He was <u>singing</u> in a car<u>toon</u>.

You have fourteen days
before lunar night turns to lunar noon.

　　　　　<u>Have</u> you <u>heard</u>, Kyle?
　　　　　He was <u>hardly</u> in a car <u>ever</u>.

I'm still ringing through loose strata.

Laika needs a lullaby and you
used to pet my dog's soft ears.

Shade

Fingernails under wallpaper
scratching sound like palpable
air, scatter-pattern of hands
behind your headboard, the face
you're sure—a third floor
window, the peripheral whisked
looking in—what don't you
believe? A boy the color
of a lightbulb cowering
in the corner of an old
hotel or rounding a wind-licked
house in full flee. Not eyes,
not corpuscles or corpses. The stain
of shape. The sand-scrubbed
rubbed-thin trace of veinery
pressed into stone. A violence
so shattering, his body not bulwark
or ballast enough, the spirit
jerks loose and imprints itself,
releasing his huddled, focused fear
like dust from a hung rug.
Skin icing over nerve, you want
to believe feeling evaporates, leaves
nothing, not even
a wet mark. Emotion a scrim
like early morning mist or just morning
touching bodies in their beds.

The Dead, Dreaming

In this half-gleam
we don't

        sleep, but glisten
continuously.
              Where the light
might

      —we catch, sheet
lifted and bit
in the pin.

Does it concern you, this
being of one body?
             Consider

hair, how much of it
is wind, how the wind
               tatters

to tendrils and the tendrils
touch.
    To be inside such

opalescence,

skin of milkglass, with inmost
listening the bridge of evening
and a child's lost progress

                    past us

disquiets.

Dreaming, her one foot
leaving, we cling.

We would air her
                    nothingness

among us, safe
        from the brightness,
                    the pulsing,

and the pocket of eggs
                    seed
deep in our teeth.

Before the flickered windows,
daily dirtying of [   ] pages,
[   ] murmured words
you've tried so hard to inherit.

Myth

She of the unwritten
question, and he who plucked
her lambent answers
                    into hymn.

Who'd twined her with a strummed
thrumming and taught
her tightening eyes how a self
from all its hemmed-in skin,
                    insistent listening,

can unhinge.
Now outside of her
                    smallness,
                    following.
She owed him

his hunger, the chance
to diminish her.
Or diminish from him, and to her

                    some air,

            the sound that flows on the grey hills
            and gathers, alluvial in rooms.

She was learning how to be
                    limitless,

a scented stain, a tarnish
wandering, child

wading for the first time eternal
into the far glittering
where light erases

this instant and the bridge to get there.

Even she did not know—
if his bodied,

from-all-the-four-corners need did not
deceive him, if his gaze straightened

and he made it back to the world he'd made
her from—if she'd let herself be

bargained,
bodied—

an empty
aerie, wind among trees.

Daphne Digging In

Tarnish-scent
of times
    skin
felt tight
and touch-shy,
       the many
buds of my body ready

       to break
under hot breath.

Rustling, heat-steeping—

this movement always
outward

    so slow
it can't be seen.

I could be swift as riverwater
or still as ground,
      and yet the feeling

that all my daily turnings
were toward a center

       I could not cull,
deeper into a self and a shell
I'd always felt but not felt flesh.

Pliant in the never-still,
susurrus as a mind that stirs

spent wings. How climbingly
the heartwood fills.

Can silence
be heard inside
                such swayings,
rapturous from a root? Bright,

a high singing in extremities,
taking me elastic,

                weightless,
wider, the clearest

                chartreuse
rinsing like a gaze.

Adam's Excuse

Every plant poised
at the point of its own
opening—petals
folded like mouse-ears
downy and thinly fleshed,
fruit hard with un-loosened juice,
every animal's eyes shallow
with un-narrowed light—
I remember the world
was new but also
unyielding. I started
performing minor
surgeries, testing
how my teeth broke skin,
how my finger slid inside
the hasp of a pea's green seam,
unclasping one by one
its tender contents.
Is it any wonder I wanted something
to bear more than the name
I gave it, why I entered her
body new as unbruised fruit
that never gathered enough
weight to fall?

Eve's Defense

Suddenly everything
    had a word. Each day
he led a new beast
    by the scruff
or muzzle, each name
    blossomed my throat
like scented air. *Tortoise,*
    mouse, horse, hare.
He'd found a way
    of living
with absence—a sound
    to summon the beast
when the beast wasn't
    there. How long,
with the sun only
    flickering
skin and breath
    without a word hard
to swallow, could I
    last without something
similar to give? I only
    wanted him to know
distance and emptiness
    answered, to show
how every word consumed
    hollows wider
at the core so soon
    the only thing you have
to spare is hunger.

Go back [

               ] to the day you turned [
to look down the hill
            you'd looked down
[   ] so far and thought,
           it turns, the road
turns, and goes.

The Names of Birds

Somehow stark
    and mysterious—as the names
        lark,
starling,
    linnet,
        swift
limn so little
    of the wheel,
        dip and tilted
drift, but twine
    bright skeins
        of air between
the plumped and heated,
    beating breast and their
        idea. Days
you savor this
    newness, walking around quiet
        as an egg, small
trapped tide rocking
    against the chitin;
        now tangible
as an emptied
    dish, now unknown,
        airy—so far
inside you it seems to sever
    galaxies
        with its beam.
Is it being up inside
    so much spent breath

that thrums each one
like a wet reed,
or the trilling
that brings a bursting
only a hollow-boned
body can answer?
All I know is, it wasn't
the faint music
of a curlew or any air
I have a name for
that cast me
outside this evening
to stand by the hedge—
as if somewhere
there is a song and senselessness
is the only way into it.

Westering

when the winter sits as if

when a wrist gives

when you pour two saucers-full for

when the sifter sticks

when the window

when drifts

when fenced-in, staked-down, full of forgetting, bent and
    kissed

when, if, then

when

when spoons tarnish

when the moon removes

when, whose

when wither isn't it—more drift, almost ash,

when half the calving's risked for fuller hands

when kindling's stacked, a packed pyramid—first fourteen,
    then thirteen inside

when itching rends a loose stitch, a stray

when the wash creaks in a cold key on the line

when to burn

when to cut what won't brown, tie two ends, haul and hold

when water seals stone to sediment, stem to picture turns

when the kettle seethes a stream on warming hands

when the birds

when rooms split light like a bent tin

when the cabinet's stacked, still damp or dripping, isn't it
    evening

when seed scatters, buckshot-strewn, threw, or through
    with, this

when shadows, parceled out from edge to edge

when by the bed the loose green is gotten

when skin

when burns raw red instead of, still

when lying quiet

when told to turn

when sighing through a reed of barbed trees, try

White Nightgown

From the split boll comes a strict
middling, an opening, combing,
drawing and roving. What the weft
won't show: scent of staircases,
windows, emptied spindles, new dust
turned on peeling wheels. Everything
before and behind her dissolving—
mist on water, salt in wind. Dissipates.
Prairie and more. Not teeth,
not chalk or plates for stays, but heat,
and mourning, and mornings—cast off
palimpsest someone seamed a body inside.
From the thickened distaff,
a second spinning, the barbed
abatis of axel-clogging wheat.
How this earth could be
so lethal and so golden, evening under her
clothes already, the companionable
kept air, dice-touch of buttons,
pleated plackets voiceless
for all their inward whisperings. If we could see:
scaffolding where a sparrow, the temporary
sentry of a crow, trellis even the wind
does not—only the strung un-green.
Not transparent, though nearly,
keeping, as she does, such light
company. Hanging from shoulders,
the scent of sunlight churning
thirst into butter, cistern of spent breath

and a clasped admission, purity
exhibiting every stain from a one-inch hem.
What is the seed that blooms inside
us such searing chambers? Buttons
for the knowing, the gathering
together by going through.
Pearl for the binding, the mulling
against oceans a silence that shines.

Testament

You're learning patterns
to tell your children: close
to the sowing and lapping

salt blue the weather's warmer;
the earth only shakes
on certain edges

of a continent long ago
cut adrift by shifting centers.
You are learning

backwards. There's hardly time.
Building houses closer
to mountains, tunneling deeper

through to new light,
you love all things
you've come closest to

owning, name
with the same thousand
sounds: the leaf you find

trembles like your own
aspen hand, the sky
remains bluer than any breath

you can't imagine. Losing
ways of speaking, turning
all tongues to one won't bring you

nearer to hearing. The trees
are breathing; the ground
is opening its mouths.

Before the scent [

                                                ]
                    of countries, palm oil and dried fish
and dusty huts, [*]*
                    dream of a whole world impossible
to wash from split, tender heels.

Gravity

Always this hunger
to claim what you love—to recover

the self that's razed
in the faced, stark blaze

of a wonder. Is it so difficult
to believe that a silt-

scoured stone radiates its own
dark beam, attracting attention

like a hard-edged magnet—
that connection of any sort

is willed from both sides
of the divide?

Once, a body, and for the scent
of that fresh-washed skin

alone (starch on white cotton
pressed with a hot, dry iron)

you offered your heart
like a tooth-ready fruit.

Once, a silkcotton
you had no hand in planting—

had only just that day laid your mat
beneath—where village women sat

resting, combing coos
in a calabash. Lying there with a book

you'd brought to this cluster
of dust-hewn huts—

a book written in sickly, small-boned
shapes they knew by sight, not sound—

you read what the native name
they'd given you—claimed

you with—meant. Who hasn't
gathered all their discontent,

set out for shores of still-more wilderness
without any wish but to find some sense

they've lost? Who hasn't pressed
through a lens toward

pin-pricks of dust-flung
light and, needing reasons for reading

meaning in that bright clutter,
invented stories for clusters

aligned to their one small point?
Understand, we don't claim our right

from precedent; all we know is something
in our earth-bound, blind bodies rings—

trampled soil across a bright ravine—
chimed by something as plain

as a paring knife sliding
through tooth-resistant skin,

the center-leaded, feathered weight
of roses cupped by hands late

in a sun-heavy summer—to find
a self newly named: a raw-skinned

death from new elements, a burning
beyond any common sense

of self, of family, of nation
—*Annihilation*

in God—in the words of that far-flung,
print-ridden tongue.

Lying beneath the tree's
thrown-open limbs, you couldn't think

how to tell the women your finding
so it might mean anything—

just listened to the high-blown,
wind-caught chatter risen

from their few free minutes—higher, higher—
ashes on the breath of fire.

Well Water

The Gambia, West Africa

Water, *jio, ndiem,*
ndox for boiling water
for steaming water
for dampening coos
after sifting. Water for loosening
creases of clothing, water
for soap soaking suds
through old thread.
Water for rinsing and
rinsing and, hanging, dripping
on chickens drinking in
puddles, sudden in sun.

Water for sprinkling
on thresholds of houses,
for holding dirt down
against sweeping or wind.
Water for wetting ears eyes
and mouth, for burnishing skin
for preparing like slaughter the body
for prayer. Water for fasting.
Water for thirsting and so, for sealing
the soul against sickness
or sin. Water for spitting—
even the lips must be wiped of all

water for drinking, for drawing
up buckets swimming with insects
and half of a lizard's
bird-severed sprig. Water
where someone's been
missing a twin and finds her
a bobbing, time-bloated bag. Water
for coffins and often for villages'
storage of stories, water like blood
feeding rivers of living
where we harvest each day
from down a dark throat.

You Were Not There

The Gambia, West Africa

Not your corrugate door they knocked on, not
your hand, your feet, through the coos
all the way out to the dust and heat-
center of a field, not your not
listening to mothers, who sat when you didn't
sit, not you watching and the string of girls
one by one unstrung, one by one to the baobab shade
to the spread *malan* to be spread. And how
many elders needed, and whether they glanced
where you weren't the stranger, would you say
                        something, would you stay
                              their hand, would you stay.

And the arms held down, you don't know, you weren't
there, they might have gripped their knees
and been willing, eager even, you don't know
what girls there grow up thinking: this is the way
to a husband, this is the way to the rest
of their lives, this is the way to be clean.
All their friends, and just one votive bleeding to keep
from feeling anything, much, ever and ever
again, and the elders watching, and the sounds
of the village, the pounding, the pounding,
and the day and their mothers, they've done this,
they're waiting, and the blanket is ready
to wrap them in, so they let go,
                        and they let
                              their letting.

Witness

For she is the day's alpha and omega:
pounding coos for breakfast while the world brightens,
walking the baby sick with *siburu* while the world darkens.
For she tells time by chores instead of sun:
five o-clock. No wind. From here, ruffled roof-edge
of corrugate, mud walls scabbed with an arm's-breadth-
worth of white-wash, last dab of what was left.
Corrugate doors propped shut with thick sticks.

Fenced-in circle of dirt where every body that's left
has left its mark—hatch-slash of claw, shuffle of thin
flip-flop, heavy hoof and pulled tire tread. Turned over bowl
rubbed through white enamel to black metal,
the artery of color. If darkness is beginning,
then never empty. If emptiness is absence,
then after ending. Most days I sit—if ending, beginning.

If beginning, the long speaking, the long throat
for warming. Whether the sky feathers
with light or indigoes the airing, the cooling
into blue view, the wide expanse, the breathing
into tops of lungs. Lines of laundry hanging, darker,
dampened sand pocked with drippings,
tattered T-shirts, shorts faded, permanently stained,
clipped in place with pink, baby-blue, sea-green,
plastic clothespins. Puddles of soap-soured ground,
handled green and purple headpans
tilted on the stoop, I am poured out like water.
For washing takes the better part of the morning

and must be finished by the dead hours.
For in the dead hours she closes her door for rest.
For I do not think she rests. For firstly she draws water.
For secondly, for thirdly, she returns to the well.
For I tire of counting but still she goes on working,
and no cosmological constant can undo movement—
Andromeda rolling towards us at 300 kilometers per second
or hauling one half minute the length of her long arms,
elbows locked, arms levered high above her head
and swaying her hips in time. For she is Awa, Sereer
for Eve. For when she looks up her eyes are hard to read.

For sometimes I see her look sideways at the sun
going down in a purple and orange sky.
For whether the sky is slate for three weeks,
or the stream speaks its gold-pebbled,
glitter-clipped babble, glassy lantern, true cage
for sudden rush to breaking, light's reliquary—
her Sereer is quick and bright as river water
after rains, and like river water her Sereer carries
bodies and earth, and obscures them all from my sight.

Most days I sit—a cheap battery's laminated paper casing,
popped off plastic cap, charcoal-colored powder insides
seeping out. Stick a child dragged and dropped,
I may tell all my bones. Were bodies just your way of staving
off questions? I want to know—how long did you think
we wouldn't notice? For her rice is sweet and not too dry.
For she borrows *neverdie* and cooks the sauce she knows I like.
For she shuffles and slaps her flip-flops to announce her arrival,
hands the bowl of hot food in and will not take thanks
or money for the labors of Allah's will.

Most days I sit. For You provide. For You provide

seldomly and at great cost. Shard of brown egg imported
from Holland, one roughly round wheel cut from a flip-flop
imported from Taiwan, pierced by half a stick axle.
Scrap of a Swedish phonebook *Bjorne Bjornestad*
Bjornested, or newspaper *Yaya Jammeh Begins GoodWill*
greased from half a buttered loaf of bread.
Yellow and red wrapper, Jumbo—*nexxna torop!*—twenty-five
bututs of beef bouillon seasoning, locust beans, dried fish
tossed in today's *mbahaal*. For food is brown or white
and brown, or brown and orange. If color
then from all colors one—in two kinds of quiet,
I sit, watching and waiting for something to pray for:

air of bread, flint of grain, fruit
like liquid light all fit inside fine as idea,
and I might miss the emptiness altogether.
Do you want to know when I first guessed?
I don't know. I don't have your knack for binding
mind and light. But what you did to the women—
(for she gets down on both knees to greet her elders)

woman with tattooed indigo
chin forget woman with bow-shaped
scar where two hooks bit in
forget woman with earlobes
stretched for more gold girl
who stains gums as her mother's
done with leftover lantern ash
forget girl with hatch-marks
etched in each temple, if she'd ever

left the village she'd read
eleven, or *equal to* turned
on its side, and in this new
naming forget women
whose bodies are a spell
against change take my forgetting
from me forget me—

fooling them with the milk
of men, the planet yet to find its own
dark orbit, internal turning—

only the men were fooled, raging
like death was something they could craft
from their raft of washed-up flesh,
as if the dark could penetrate
every cell. For she sits in the dark to shell groundnuts,
cracks with a quick flick of the wrist and a twist of fingers.
For I can neither experience nor describe the form
which meets me but only body it forth.

For I can sometimes make her laugh and she laughs
like a small girl.
For she has a small girl who lives in another village.
For she has two other children buried before her.
For she hauls her son up by the arm and carries
his limp body to bed.
For she is the last by the fire, pours water
over embers to make coal for tomorrow's ironing,
to make orange, the ripened rind of red-
shift, how quickly galaxies from a fixed point
recede, the risen hissing, the turning under tongue.

Maybe you'd had enough of voices
blurring with your one unwavering silence.
For often she says nothing. Knowledge?
That's just the print-setter's term for having
sense, and we preferred to know
the world more ways than through the five
limitations of our bodies, naming and renaming.
When our catalog was exhaustive—for water
is *water*, also *jio*, also *ndox*, also *ndiem*,

also an odorless, tasteless, very slightly compressible
liquid oxide of hydrogen H_2O which appears
bluish in thick layers, freezes at $0°C$ and boils
at $100°C$, is a poor conductor of electricity and a good
solvent, descends from the clouds as rain, forms streams,
lakes and seas, a major constituent
of all living matter—we thought
we'd have reached you. But here is no water
but only rock, rock and no water
and the sandy road, the road winding drip drop
drip drop drop drop drop but there is
no water and we haven't crafted an ocean
with our small collection of sounds, words
just divisions rooting us deeper in dirt,
roads that fade or deepen depending on the season,
depending on how many feet trample to, or past,
the fallow fields. The air breathes upon us here
most sweetly, as if it had lungs and rotten ones.
We want the brimming nothing back you tricked us from,
and we don't care how many worlds we have to destroy:

you who pushed through hips of hill dust
you who rose through mouth bloom of dust
you who blew apart far from the hole
How were your dust-veins slickened to blood
When were your dust-lungs caged against air
Why were your dust-teeth sharpened to stone
What will your dust-dreams make of your waking
with two feet for tracking the hollow down
two nostrils for finding the hollow ground
two ears for ringing against hollow ground
two eyes for watering the hallowed ground
two hands for smoothing the hollow down
when the hollow is found.

There—listen. Are you near
enough to hear this breath of sense,
this garbled trilling of body
mimicking reed? We were mixed
in gas and granite with you
in the beginning, and beyond this
recognition and rush towards more
forced air, detritus of helium,
deuterium by which we measure
quasars and cosmic background radiation
variations the seeds from which galaxies grow,
enough undetectable dark matter to bring
us to the border between expanding
emptiness and slowing slowly towards reverse,
the air's the sound of stopping, the world a force
pressing harder in the deeper you sink.

Before the man with the scars

                        and still sparse hair who reached

across your cup of green tea, pressed

                        the enameled pin into your palm

and said, here, it is yours, we

                  [   ] had

radiation sickness.

City of Water

If you drop light on the city center,
    there are many uses for hair.
The air is forced out, but soon,
    pillows, paintbrushes, and if
it must wash back creating hurricane winds,
    you can find any still flying nests.
Sports field come crematorium, come,
    you can't always trust the all-clear
sweet potato farm to feed the citizens.
    By all accounts at detonation, light
if it crawls, please, it isn't rice
    that feels like a pin-cushion.
Then fire, altitude of high ash content,
    the map a bullet-wound radiating
black rain. If you find yourself running
    from the hypocenter, approximate damage.
On a bridge it's best not to faint.
    Shoes can be lost in melting asphalt.
Someone might put you on a truck.
    It may be hard to distinguish males from females
with the other unmoving. If they do,
    even in the City of Water you
hope you fall off. Your best bet,
    beg for what could carry the invisible further
to survive the first few days, a soldier
    into your bloodstream, cells, the tiny
unearthing your accidental pulse,
    units of bodies, our heirs.

Current

Vice defense minister on the commission announced we have reason on the third Sunday of the second millennium polls indicate Tuesday talks resumed over the no-fly zone twenty-three civilians negotiate the Dow Jones if they are not prepared yesterday when separatists say they won't wait outside fighting 5000 demonstrators police estimate broke out approaching from the north a few showers this is all things 55 degrees and partly local eyewitnesses say the destruction they haven't gotten only on the black market doesn't know postponed medical supplies including a third floor blanket of smoke resumed the national average clearly we need decisive refugees gathered the next few days continuing to monitor we don't anticipate at this time at least a dozen school children.

Days After

Let me
                    just say

            the ugliest
thing, let me
                    just
say, I am
I
am grateful

everyone I
                    know

                              I am
                              keeping in a pen

            of exhaustion, a tenderness
                              that feels

like greed the muscled,

            flat pads of
                    that man's hands, this
woman's thin wrists

                    I am holding up the grey-
                              white shape
of my life lived and finished it fits

                    and unlike
        a mask
        the eyes are

the only part left not cut
                        out
                                anyone

whose name
                I know, I want
                to stop and grip
        by the shoulders,
                                tilt

my chin to aim my eyes more precisely

in and ask
                        How are you

                            still here

History

Our most persistent nightmare
is of aftermath and a child
patrolling the silent shells
of buildings, the city a kingdom
of loose curtains, eyeless high-rises,
and nowhere a home for smoke.
Understand, it's not as if
we left him there. His shoes
are sturdy and he has no need
for food. If I gave him a curfew
and nothing else, not even a pack
of matches, you wouldn't worry.
You'd watch him lay hands
against the flanks of buildings,
watch him turn to the white-eyed
shapes of statues and give comfort
with his permanence—the way
the living watch the grieving
and weigh them down with fingerprints,
with a blood contract for more
stories and blankets of wild breath.

Before the scent of other bodies
             on you, sour milk of children,
curdled seed of men,
             before the scent[   ]

Vows

In the dream
worth keeping
we're watching
both windows,
view of constant
tenuousness, branches
quivering with just-
landing or the push
preceding flight, who
can say. We're told
they mate for life;

we would too, if
we had wings.
But how, when so much
surrounding us
is ground, meaning
once even this
stillness we walk on
was grinding skin,
saliva, bone,
and leaf and the chaff
is older than any
standing.

Sonnet

This child wants to know which
way the wind is. And whether
he's a seedling or a star.
Will he be a someday where
his eyes might. Gently lift,
and all the songs I single,
string with please. Oh, little luck
of my nothing. Little you who,
heart of my parting, night-hob
listening with fists to his lips.
You are a hard garden. You will not
be season, sealed to blooms. If I knew
the way to be here, I would send
you a sliver, lever to a who.

She Wearies of Wise Children

All night they bring her permission
slips, in their bloodless hands, roses
from neighbors' trellises. They ask her
to anchor the bunched headiness
in her hair. They speak in a flurry
of wings. They want to be outside,
they want to be lifted by the wind
and carried. They want TV and speed.
To feel the words like credits
roll from their tongues as they read.
They can spell *their*. They know *ow*
is spelled *oh you*. They see silence
is something to be shouted
into, a space where nothing you can do
scatters absence, leaves a lasting.
Sometimes when I cry I taste
my tears and it tastes good.
They pedal their gleaming through streets.
They hug like hiding behind a tree.

Late April

teachers lined beneath
   low cloud and a high
brightness skittering how like ethereal
   litter the wind-caught coats the clattering
jackets flash of red of blue
   twittering of a gull's under-
wing the jumped-from swing
   jerking like dropped chain there
are those who say grounded
   caged and clipped but battering
against fences just now everything
   can be shaken eyes horizoned
and still the world
   whirling the axis-tilted tether-
ball scribing ellipses

Go back, you remember, the way is open,
            though memory has not fastened

its teeth [

                                  ]

[   ] to borrow
            from other's memories

Urban

You are watched
and that starts to feel

significant living in
a valley where every hectare

of mountain is inhabited memories
of grids trace someone

else's circuits and always you
are approaching a center some

pulse to keep time with what words
have drifted past you and not

caught laddered girders of ghost
rungs everywhere is right

angle silver glitter
sting and it can all come

down because metal is an element
we taste in the molten

ore of our bodies any
window is a mirror given

enough light and what you miss
are your earlier versions without

reflection a frame to turn our
raised cups paging through papers

into stills of a time too
shining to inhabit or return to

and is now there are those
you can never again approach

talk to touch and glass
is the coldest reminder of this

Definition

1: the bed after either has left it. e.g. the light, the shapes
in the flat-sheet. indentations. soft fossil marks.
2: to have or want to have. to imagine in violet corridors.
3: to reduce in intensity. to lavender.
e.g. the air three days after the house was shut; not
three years—the air itself an inhabitant;
not three lifetimes—even the air has moved on.
e.g. a full nothing. <she ~ed most in the mornings.>
4: to wake from. to polish the edge of dream.
also, to see oneself in an eye, to shrink
with exposure. to wither
in skin. to retreat into bone.
5: to shine, as one scoured by some clear substance.
6: to say the exact opposite. to sully pages. to idle.
to walk, esp. when pines bear white branches, flaked fractal
patterns, esp. when
7: to desire to come, go, or be.
8: to follow prints, evidence
of presence and passing. <he is ~ed>
9: to hunger. to redefine hunger as something not tied
to the body. to murmur, to fail to fill, *esp. in desired*
or customary grace.
see INTERIOR.

Atlantean

Every lintel peers
at its own reflection,

and deeper, what
the room once dreamed

it sheltered.
Is there any sound

more leveling than
a house closed around

the *clip, clip*
of a faucet long silent,

submerged? Everything
becomes a dripping point:

saturated curtains,
tipped china finger

of a soggy doll.
That sound? It's the pipes

giving up their long hold,
groan of a wrenched railing,

metal throats filling
with a new equilibrium.

Oh, water is no known
emotion. Like sleeplessness,

it seeps and is never
still. This is all any of us

wants—to be changed
by something utterly

outside and entered,
spores tracing lace

on every surface,
some substance finding

reliquaries inside
we didn't know

were there. The thousand
tongues of books

swollen and bled
of their dialects.

And when you go back,
what do you claim?

The lost versions
of loved faces, the lead

soldiers dear to one
who died before you knew

him? Everything,
everything—stray hairs

from the hairbrush,
receipts. The shape a head

left in the pillow lingers.
Rowing a skiff between

street signs, it's hard
to know which house

from half-way up.
You could be

dreaming. Your vaporous,
discarded hours

retreating into the bones
and staves of the rooms.

The trace of brine to tell you,
below here, it's all lost.

Anywhere you touch
the wall, it weeps.

Weather

What the rain erases
from a safe distance isn't

worth mentioning. Dishes
rinsed and dripping, still

door on its hinges, glass
tightening in panes.

This isn't accusation; it's only
we keep wanting beyond

all breadth and sense.
A woman stands by bare

windows, outside whitening
under the steady fall of her

attention. Even memory,
that ticking, how-long-gone

longing erases the direction
of weather. Even waking.

If we have souls we want them
to look like this: ground,

and not-quite-sky and light.

Going back, the beginning's always stitched
                    with other stories, and yours is no
beginning but [

                    ]light,
devouring light [

Unaccounted-for Storm

30,000 feet

We are not meant for this
passage, and feel it

                    in throat-
caught air, skin tensile
as thinking
            fissures wedged between

thresholds, the only ones
high enough to mark
                the dark,

dropped cloth of our own faint,
lost constellations—

so much loose nothing wanting

story,
        moon-roil dissolving
tall coral cumulus,
                flutter-pulse

from this moving corona making
vein-work and cloud-shadow
              seen.

Etymology of Evening

Not darkening, but balancing, some thing

weighed against its absence and dissolving

from a source that can't be seen. The cool

of sheltered beds, the shortening

of corridors. And the words we circle in this

leveling—*wisteria, lilac*—resting in eddies.

This is where what you can't horizon

increases incrementally. The gift is, in this world

no hole is dense enough to swallow

semblance, the field of wildflowers blurring

around a rumor of hues. *Evening*, as dependable

as circumstance, as the assurance that

all sorrows, all joys are exactly divisible

in pairs. Any number of atoms seeping

toward a moment of precision when nothing

can pierce the drowsing houses. So everywhere

and even-handed—the restlessness, the centerless

days. In the hour when grips loosen

their hold and breath has a presence no suddenness

can disperse, bathwater's drawn, a hand

rends a hem, and *when* is not a question

you care to counter.

Monologue

Go back before the body you lay down beside the man who
borrows your breath at night and leaves you, you want to say,
breathless, before the dream of falling, drowning, drifting,
dream of your life as you've lived it. Before the flickered
windows, daily dirtying of teaspoons, the pages turned over
murmured words you've tried so hard to inherit. Before the
scent of other bodies on you, sour milk of children, curdled
seed of men, before the scent of countries, palm oil and dried
fish and dusty huts, tang of soy and seaweed, dream of a whole
world impossible to wash from split, tender heels. Before the
man with the scars and still sparse hair who reached across
your cup of green tea, pressed the enameled pin into your palm
and said, *here, it is yours, we used to wear it when we had radiation
sickness.* Go back, you remember, the way is open, though
memory has not fastened its teeth to the day you turned from
the garden to look down the hill you'd looked down every
summer so far and thought, it turns, the road turns, and goes.
Go, though now you start to borrow other's memories, back
to red striped wallpaper stretching floor to ceiling, like vocal
chords screaming at the door to be let loose. Going back, the
beginning's always stitched with other stories, and yours is no
beginning but one sentence no one writes in the book of a
people making decisions to drop light, devouring light on a
city, searing one hand permanent against stone, to pack souls
like spices in crates over oceans, or send shuttles to the bright,
pocked surface of night's eye. Keep going, you cannot claim a
clean beginning anymore than you can say how far back your
life is tied to, how far back you want to stop and start the story.

Aquifer

Nothing tastes like what it comes from,
meaning water, whose taste is action,
is the throat opening like ground
washed in light. What has happened
to the rooms moved through in cold pipes,
and the metal pipes, and first the dirt
or the word and the worm
and the sand that is the conscience
of the aquifer, allowing not even drops
to move through but moisture grain
to grain to deeper ground like an infant
passed between hands passes deeper
into breathing, meaning dying, meaning
nothing is all beginning. Even this poem,
passed between words, meaning
dumb hope something will be said
to make the effort worth finishing.
A friend was telling about a fight
that broke out in her class and the moment
she mentioned the girl saying, "What
did you say?" to the boy, I had
assumptions. The girl, who had been speaking
up all her life and wasn't constrained,
as her white classmates were, by the need
to be submissive and decorative,
was black. And the boy, who sank deeper
in his seat, having realized long ago
that school would be the one place
where being his mother's son would get him

nothing, and who, not very bright, resented
the necessity for work, and school, was white.
That's just one ugly way I bring the world
to bear on strangers. We all do it.
The man I loved in college saying, "Someday
when I hear you're marrying someone else,
I'll think it's wrong. I'll always think
you're wrong." All his dissolved feeling
like silt in my blood. We carry
words, their origins and ideas, rain
disappearing, water *like snakes,*
slithering to find a hole in the ground,
and my student who handed me these words
carrying the one word I gave him back, beyond knowing
what a *poet* is. Meaning water,
which isn't eternal, but the thirst, which has water
in it by being absent the moment you say it.

Notes

· "Myth" is based, of course, on Rilke's "Orpheus. Eurydice. Hermes." I also had Sam Reed's poem "Pluviana" in my head, which reads "She's trying to be more nameless."
· "The Names of Birds" is for Katy, in memory of Gypsy.
· In "The Names of Birds," the phrase "faint music" is borrowed from Robert Hass. Some syntax is also borrowed from Stephen Mitchell's translation of Rilke.
· In "Well Water" and "Witness," the words jio, ndiem, and ndox are the Fula, Mandinka and Wolof words for "water".
· In "Witness," "Sereer" represents a West African language and ethnic group; "Yaya Jammeh" is the current president of The Republic of The Gambia.
· In "Witness" the following lines are borrowed from other sources:

   -"I may tell all my bones" and "I am poured out like water" from The Song of Songs.
   -"For I can neither experience nor describe the form which meets me but only body it forth" from Buber's *I and Thou*.
   -"an odorless, tasteless, very slightly compressible... a major constituent of all living matter" from *Webster's Ninth Collegiate Dictionary*.
   -"Here is no water but only rock... but there is no water" from Eliot's "The Wasteland."
   -"The air breathes upon us here most sweetly, as if it had lungs and rotten ones" from Shakespeare's *The Tempest*.

· "Witness" borrows stylistically in part from Smart's "Jubilate Agno."

· "Selenographia" is for Kyle Patton, 1996-2004.
· "City of Water" takes most of its images and information from John Hersey's *Hiroshima* and The Hiroshima Peace Culture Foundation's *Eyewitness Testimonies; Appeals From the A-Bomb Survivors.*
· In "She Wearies of Wise Children," the lines in italics belong to Yareli Franco.
· "Atlantean" is for my father.
· In "Definition," lines in italics are quoted from *Webster's Ninth Collegiate Dictionary*.
· In "Aquifer" the lines in italics were first uttered by Aaron Miller.

Apprentice House Press
Loyola University Maryland

Apprentice House is the country's only campus-based, student-staffed book publishing company. Directed by professors and industry professionals, it is a nonprofit activity of the Communication Department at Loyola University Maryland.

Using state-of-the-art technology and an experiential learning model of education, Apprentice House publishes books in untraditional ways. This dual responsibility as publishers and educators creates an unprecedented collaborative environment among faculty and students, while teaching tomorrow's editors, designers, and marketers.

Outside of class, progress on book projects is carried forth by the AH Book Publishing Club, a co-curricular campus organization supported by Loyola University Maryland's Office of Student Activities.

Eclectic and provocative, Apprentice House titles intend to entertain as well as spark dialogue on a variety of topics. Financial contributions to sustain the press's work are welcomed. Contributions are tax deductible to the fullest extent allowed by the IRS.

To learn more about Apprentice House books or to obtain submission guidelines, please visit www.apprenticehouse.com.

Apprentice House
Communication Department
Loyola University Maryland
4501 N. Charles Street
Baltimore, MD 21210
Ph: 410-617-5265 • Fax: 410-617-2198
info@apprenticehouse.com • www.apprenticehouse.com

www.ingramcontent.com/pod-product-compliance
Lightning Source LLC
Chambersburg PA
CBHW072046040426
42447CB00012BB/3039